SONGS FOR MARGARET CRAVENS

USPOCO BOOKS, a non-profit publisher, is a division of us poetry company.

All rights reserved under International and Pan-American Copyright Conventions. Published in the United States by **USPOCO BOOKS**, Asheville, NC.

uspocobooks@gmail.com

ISBN **978-0983306207**
Library of Congress Control Number:

FIRST EDITION

Cover Art by Barrett Travis

SONGS FOR MARGARET CRAVENS

Chris Wong

USPOCO BOOKS

ASHEVILLE, NC

NEW AMERICAN POETRY SERIES
NUMBER TWO

USPOCO BOOKS

Asheville, NC

Author's Note:

Although she was raised in Indiana, Margaret Cravens lived much of her adult life in Paris. Despite limited financial means, she supported Ezra Pound in his writings and research from the fall of 1911 until her death by suicide in June of 1912.

This poem uses as its primary source Omar Pound and Robert Spoo's edition of a collection of letters entitled *Ezra Pound and Margaret Cravens: A Tragic Friendship, 1910-1912* (Duke University Press 1988). Brackets are my own remarks, but all misspellings and parenthetical clarifications that appear in epigraphs are sic.

For Ben and Jessica and Barrett and Brett
For my mother and my father
and most of all for Alison and for my brother
without whose love this book would not exist

It is the blight man was born for.
It is Margaret you mourn for.
—Hopkins

I.

St. George slaying a dilapidated dragon.
—EP

I haven't seen sun rise or set in months.
I've read your book of letters, Margaret, now
so many times. I still can't tell you what it means,
or whether what it had to say, I knew.

On every night the walls without a face.
What April had — or so she said — there was no cure.
(You notice every poem I write takes place
inside a room? So why should anybody care?)

In this room the walls grow increasingly wide.
How did April, Margaret, get here, where I am?
I lived with three friends, all of whom have wives.
I sensed a part of me was growing part of them,

alone among my friends. We curled, as two dogs
curl around each other, once. But then she broke
away from me. I tried to lose her. Drink. Then drugs.
Then, searching for new poems, I found your book.

And it seemed that you and April were the same.
Could you show me where she drew her memories
and what of the evening settles in that sum
and in what empty glass she left me mesmerized?

And what is the big reveal as shadows wane?
I found in your letters where you said to him:
My loneliness is not that I'm alone
but someday that I must and will and am.

II.

There is no need you too will understand or you would not have been near me.
—Margaret Cravens

and the aspects of the flame are of a great resound
(orders of magnitude arranged from "insignificant"
to "a grain of sand"). The sound of fire is like the sound
of thunder. Both bring ghosts, magnificent

across the heavens, dancing in the toothless snap of twigs
and then: the flash of lightning.
Fires, foremost, bring our circle out, in rings
among the night. The first fire even came from thunder, latening

to hand-cut stacks of logs, which bring clouds of their own.
I met a girl once, passing on the early streets of Madison,
up from Indiana. She was April. It was Halloween
and though we were drunk and bed-bound soon

she wouldn't let me fuck her till I told her all
I knew of death. And then we burned three candles
down to glass as framed bolts forked and fell
against the sky. We found ourselves rekindled

in my rented room, found sleep there, wandered
one another's bodies, feeling grim and wise
in ways of small and happy death. We wondered
if anything else in the world was burning. There was—

III.

[Swinburne]'s vision of our marvellous vitality, of our power for survival! Oh well — example — your power of surviving this utterly endless epistle. The gods avail you.
—EP

The woman climbs the stairs. Draws back
her hair among her ears. And then the use
of the narrative *you* becomes a roadblock
wherein the reader's puzzled by the *you's* —

Both are obviously a woman. But do both
occupy the same apostrophe? Same value?
Can one be exchanged for the next? What math
might solve this? Subtraction? And — what volume

of emotion can be contained in this small vessel?
John Wilkinson told me a stanza's a jar which holds
what can't be held. My stanzas will in this way bristle.
The weight of your contents will be spilled

on to the next. The woman walks the stairs
having called on her lover hours before her death.
Which you will I use when her face disappears
into that gasping, final, room-filled breath?

IV.

I wonder have you arms wherewith to slay.
—EP

The timing of the medusa in the shield
of Perseus had left me dull and blind,
a pillar of limestone, marble, shale
in my own image. Dull beer, blonde

in a fluted glass, and memories of France
and frantic streets — judgments of Paris
etched on February's Gorgon face.
Sprinklings of you against a porous

topcoat. Petrifice. That looking backward.
Slow clouds of salt through an empty sky
so full of thoughts. That looking-back word
you pronounced with firm lips, pink and dry:

Remember? arched across that wooden table
stained dark brown to seem antique. The cold, thin
band around your thumb, faint stubble
of your ankle brushing mine — even then

I knew the distance years had kept
between us. Even as your glance, all sly,
hides failures of the past which you encrypt —
I wonder have you arms wherewith to slay.

V.

I wrote to Ezra as he will be very sorry, as I believe he tried more than the rest to help her and develop her. But she has had these attacks already often and it was but a matter of years.
—Walter Rummel

You, little kitten, all across three states
that guard you from me: you are mine.
Always afloat atop the dizzying straits
that channel us among the rocks—I mean,

we're brought to where the current takes us
quite against our wills, my little cat.
The rhythms of the motions of the world, they tax us,
and I'm not quite certain at this moment that

the depths of hard despair are yours alone—
O kitty cat across from me three states—
when I think of you. What was that line
from Hector? Oh: *There is no man outlives the fates.*

VI.

oh real breath with the blossoms in it.
—EP

He was right, you know. Your soft
and sacred arms, pale bruised
and frail are whatsoever safe.
Once pulled me closer to your breast.

Departed love. I still could slip
my arm around you if the world
would wait. Could fall to you as sleep
falls into night, dark, walled

as silence. I couldn't calm the voices
though they urged me, in their stillness, to depart.
Through repetition, you became my vices,
rippling, and of a slow-mouthed port

where I am washed but not redeemed.
Sad brown eyes (repeated from a dream).
They should have been enough. But it was doomed.
I left southbound on yet another train.

VII.

This is the only stationery which "sells itself" at the only convenient tobacco shop — it says "Eleganza" on the packet, so, for its ambitions pardon its defects.
—EP

Behind the increasing fog, the day
and where the day will take me looms.
It's not so long before we both will die,
though long in the life of water blooms

or mayflies, or dog day locusts — from late
mid-afternoon to dark, I heard their whine,
those fractured lovers in the branches. They alight
to wander the sweat of heat and the brine

of rain which silenced them. And now I drive
twelve hours across the states to pay you visit.
It isn't so long we both remain alive.
I hope it's long enough to see you. Is it?

VIII.

I am swigging Hippocrene to beat all hell.
—EP

The sun begins to squat upon the air
and I find new ways to stumble
home by summer mornings, where
I wake to angels atop a thimble

dancing their loud and clanging songs
to wake me to the hangovers of day.
Your phone call woke me there, among
the weeds and reeds of rubbish. So away

I tucked my phone, returned to sleep,
thinking I would call you later.
But you had promises to keep
and a simplicity to neatly shatter.

Some suicides, their friends insist, could not
have killed themselves *that way*, too glad
to be alive to slip, let's say, a knot
around their neck and come unglued

from wherever they'd found themselves stuck
by any god or no god they imagined.
Yet, you went and walked beside that lake,
turning in your head that broken engine

of your metaphysics. Late that evening
your father calls and tells me where you are.
The distance between us is an uneven thing.
If you must leave, don't let me be so far.

IX.

*Their exchange went unrecorded; what impressed Walter was
Margaret's serenity. The next day, after the bewildering news had
reached him, he would comment that she "called on me several hours
before her death and seemed so quiet and so kind, that I don't under-
stand a thing."*
—OP and RS

On discovering her suicide (both
Margaret's and the other girl's) I wept
not. Only sighed, and, in that breath,
smoked down a cigarette and wrapped

my mind around these women I was not.
April who survived. You, Margaret, who
have died. Considered how pristine and neat
if April would have died, yet full of woe

and whether that woe is lessened now, if I
am cheapened in my grief by how unfair
to place myself beside her act. Another sigh,
another cigarette. And lo, the night grows far.

X.

Its dangerous in dealing with an imaginative mind, this sort of ambiguity.
—EP

I dreamed I came to an abandoned temple
and stood among the ruined pillars.
Is this where I've arrived by your example,
left alone to wander each night's pallor?

There I stood, alone and desperate
for even a slight cool breeze to stir
some dust up here among the desolate.
The air was still. I climbed a stair

that led to nowhere. Through a cloud
I turned and stared in back of me
and found the stairs had all been cleared
to nothing. There I stood, halfway.

Would it be too simply put if now I said
that I awoke then, unaware
of where I was and had been? But I did.
And then returned to sleep. I climbed a stair.

XI.

I haven't told you yet that I like your poems. I don't need to. I think
Margaret Cravens must have.
— Alice Corbin Henderson

Where did I find you, girl, I once —
the act of the mind in the act of the mind —
from what other source, or whence
did I find you, girl? I find

in the narrative arc, the narrative sense,
I found you, girl, I found you at the last
and only in the days invented since
did I find you girl I lost.

Too late in the sense of: "O there Is A God,"
and how all ends in flat rejection if
there is any dispute whether God is good,
whether Margaret's words are stolen, or rather of

my many selves as I divest myself, aplomb
as the plan detaches from itself,
and I am left with this very modern poem.
That is — in trinity — reiterated, reified, unsafe.

Me, April, Margaret. Words I found.
If two points detach from the original line. . .
And then this long poem is my only friend
and O the days grow fast, and sharp, and mean.

XII.

There is in the middle of your last letter a long passage which I believe contains many deep philosophical conclusions & some revelations of your inmost character. I am quite unable to decipher the passage.
—EP

How sinister and selfish I awoke.
How plain and agonizing was the day.
How flat and clean the sunrise broke
to spread the shadows out along its way.

And the news arrives that April lives
though to me the morning feels the same
as if she'd died. Whatever force forgives
such thoughts, I offer it the shame

of having thought them. Though to me it is.
The same. She sleeps away the week.
We can't speak. I can't offer her a kiss.
That she lives reminds me I'm as weak

as she was, out along the shore,
throwing her body over, to be fished
from the water's depths. What's more,
the unavoidable fact: she said she wished

never to see me again, and the guilt
that accompanies the fact: I left
her first. She left me last. She spilt
the last of all her many tears. I wept.

XIII.

I go to get drunk on Sirmione sun for the last time this month.
— EP

Midnight in Covent Gardens we glided,
the professor's son and the carpenter's daughter
and me. Outside the moonlight's wings were gilded.
She sang: *Does anyone remember laughter?*

And laughter. O those cobbled streets shook
with music. The basement at Notting Hill Arts
held us in the arms of song. By that cool brook,
the Serpentine, we walked all spring. Our hearts

unburdened then, us three — the carpenter's girl,
the professor's boy, and me. Then one by one
they left me, flocked against the sky like gulls.
The professor died, and so his son was gone,

to disappear forever to his family's side. My love,
she drifted slower. I sank to drink and pills
which helped April drift. Which helped her leave
for good, though we had our returns. The pull

was unavoidable. She was the best I've known.
And the streets of Soho by neon were bright
as if through drunken tears in the glare of noon —
a washed-out lens flare, silhouettes by starlight.

These are temporal things I've tried to escape.
Our love was ending. It was going to end.
Even in the best of skies, the pale, clear cup
of moonlight in her palm was going to bend.

I whispered: *You are gorgeous in this light.*
And the professor's son just rolled his eyes.
When I see her again, her smile is not so bright.
The time and the place and the moon were our disguise.

XIV.

The "Weaver of Beauty" was Margaret Cravens, whose last act but one on the night of her suicide was to play one of these songs on her piano.
— OP and RS

Let me tell the story of her last
day on earth. April woke. Began
to think of things that could be lost.
Things she might not regain.

She told me a few, post-mortem,
on the phone: how easily her name
had been remade, and martyred
by an ex-lover (me), hell-bent to blame

her for the trivialities of loss,
how easily his (my) sentences unwove
her sense of self. Had made her less.
That was one thing. The other, I strove

to understand but failed: The *thought*,
she murmured. *Thought*. She kept
repeating. It was the *thought*. They *thought*
she was alive now. But she slept

for nearly a week until she finally awoke.
The hospital floor is neat. Her sheets
are blue and stained. Still weak,
they bring her soup, they give her shots,

that same slow drip. I sit and hold
the hand I once dragged through Soho
laughing, cursing the night to hell,
slipping in our sandals. That soft glow

of lights in the puddle of the curb,
the fluorescent off her cheeks.

Soft. Still. She lies in this pitiful crib,
its bitter blue. Some white dust chalks

the rails and I want to throw up.
But I won't throw up. I'll only wait
for her to wake and, with trembling lips,
tell me why and how and for what

she could walk beside Lake Mendota
and throw herself to the tide (do lakes
have tides? Does it matter?) O daughter
of the carpenter, what flat and deepened stakes

had they driven through your palms
to make your blood — staunch, black —
refuse to flow? All I have for you are poems,
poems which ebb in your presence. Grow slack

and incomplete. You say: *I too am incomplete*
when your voice is finally found. But what remains
of the you I loved? Do you hear me? I want to explode.
What will I do if you do this again?

XV.

If your really in a slough of miserability I could come over for a week
if it would in any way divert you.
—EP

An anchor, sank foot deep and wide.
If you were what he said you said
(she yammers, cheap red wounds of words),
parsed and over-parsed, instead

of what you claimed to be, I once
was a beautiful worm. An anchor
sank foot deep and wide. You wince
and explain how once you cried

for a lover who was me and whom
you abandoned, and who was devastated
the day when, northbound, you left home.
You are the sort of woman, understated

and refined. The sort of woman
who defines herself the way she wades
across a conversation, woven
in the thread of whoever waits

forever for her return (to me). An
anchor sank foot deep and wide. You are
that sort. And I, the sort of man
who lets her get away with things. Like war.

XVI.

Hats form an important part of "the woman question."
—Dorothy Shakespear

It was the year I cut out half my mind
in case there might be demons. Paris was a maze —
unswept, uncanvassed on that mound
at Sacre Coeur, where on the hill I gazed

over thatch-roofed streets. If I'd had a guide
to Montmartre — someone like you, O Margaret, raven-
haired and pale — to lead me down that grade,
away from the tourist spots to those uneven

roofs below, the jigsaw puzzle of that city might
have solved itself for me, in the less than neon glow
of night. Perhaps French-speaking passersby I'd meet
wouldn't regard me with such halting, slow,

unfriendly smiles. Paris was d'Orsay, though, not
those houses down the hill. Not the dismal. The pristine,
sterile, un-gleamed majesty. And not
gray mornings in these scenes that I'd been pressed in

alone, all cold and gloom, alone at a wooden table
sipping Earl Gray at some cafe I can't afford.
It was the year I cut out half my mind, unable
to please otherwise the gods. Half-dead, afeared

of what would be. And I remember: Venus de Milo.
Aphrodite in December — perfect, unencumbered
torso. And I thought of April's arms — calm, pillow-
soft. Paris in the winter. Snow. The slumber.

I remember missing her. And I remember wavering.
I remember Plaze de Republique. And I remember
waking alone on starched sheets, alone and shivering
against a gentle wind. Yes I remember Paris. I remember —

XVII.

*This isn't a letter — merely a scrawl. . .I shall write a saner note
when I emerge from this atmosphere of arrangement & expediency.*
—EP

The first panic attack I read desperately "Ship of Death,"
as if there were words that could calm my shortened breath.
While my roommates were out, drinking themselves to death
I wondered why "death" rhymed so easily with "breath."

The apples will fall as I crumble. And thoughts of death
creep like fog against my window where my breath
makes clouds. Still visible, which means a lack of death
though at any moment they uncloud. And breath

is no easier to come by now than respite from death.
Slick silence. No passing cars, not even the breath
of another soul. I drag a finger through "Ship of Death,"
incant the words and I am soothed. Under my breath

I chant and am soothed. *Piecemeal the body dies* its death —
words which ease all worries but of shortened breath
as I gasp and, breathless, plot details of my death.
There are several casual evils. The worst of them is death.

XVIII.

However if we poke the white wooly elephant long enough it may
squeak. (This note is not on any account to be delivered to the com-
missioners for public sanity.)

Aloha. And the gods ~~save~~ *avail you.*
—EP

Moving these keys beneath my hands
I feel like Chopin. Know how Chopin must
have felt. Performing. Not composing. And I understand
her suicide. Not its composition. No, not most

things of it. But, the constant thing to be performed.
The way a pilot feels as landing gear
becomes his legs. The way the question is framed—
Where we depart to. Consider: Gare

du Nord: *The platform says "ladies,"* a girl exclaims.
Her brother, facing opposite: *The word*
is "gentlemen." They're both wrong. These are only names.
The place they have arrived is Gare du Nord.

XIX.

At about half past seven the rain let up sufficiently for her to take
her leave.
— OP and RS

More considerations: why would she
have left all this or wanted to? O, and was
her act some flat rejection of just *me*
or of the world at large? O I am wise

because she called me wise, but that
is just another way that she misjudged
the world. See, I have spent too long in thought
pondering what long unsettled grudge

she might have kept (and I found many)
but in summation there is just the act
(although one method seems as good as any).
What can it show me of the world she lacked

that she would throw herself into that water?
I remember she told me she'd never read *Hamlet*
but I've read *Hamlet* and I told her after
class one day how Ophelia's death seems amplest

among the wealth of sadness in the play. The prince
was just intelligent enough that, self-involved
as he might be, we still afford a minor wince
upon his death. But O the girl! The girl he loved

only once or never, who threw herself away
to sink among the wretched depths — O her we fear,
that such a thought might, in our subconscious, stay
and at such moments of great peril, steer

us to the water's edge until we can't be held
responsible for our own acts. Yes, here
I find great fault with *Hamlet*, that I have recalled

Ophelia's death. The death I read to her.

XX.

But it had been only one frustration among many, and she had
always considered her friendship with him too valuable to ruin with
an open declaration.
—OP and RS

Yet another inquiry to yet another boss
who'd never have me. April, if you could
see these rejections with which I've been blessed
would you no longer dream to have been dead?

April, don't tell me again that I'm a writer,
when no man alive will pay me to write.
I'm not qualified even to be a starving waiter.
I can't get my red and white wine pairings right.

Remember the night you told me, wailing,
all your failures, weeks before you drowned?
I hung up the phone and gazed up at the ceiling
and thought of all the loose white pages strewn

beneath my desk, where all the words collect
their dust. O April, best lost love of mine, if only
you had known how little of the world's respect
I have myself, would you have felt less lonely?

XXI.

*If she'd but go [to Paris] more lightly, go for a lark in learning; go
without pretence, without the disturbing confounding of mere good
taste with talent. It makes for disillusionment, and it means coming
back to a home grown dull.*
—OP and RS

I need to be grounded. I need myself to be grounded.
I need to retreat to my dim, brown room to write.
I need the air-conditioned buzz, the keyboard pounded
in cacophonies of white noise. And I need my cat

to leave the room so no eyes left will stare,
reminding me how grounded I already am.
I need to be a dying, distant star
whose light, merely visible, lies beyond our aim.

I need to be astronaut to that star. I need
for no one ever to have died, O Margaret Cravens.
I need the human race to not undo itself. Indeed,
I need for you to not have had-got-even

with the poet who had left you. And I need my girl
not to had-got-even with me. That death by water.
April, dead. And what I need most is not to lack her gall.
And I need to decide what I will do without her.

XXII.

People are a rarity — but they are that anywhere.
—EP

The night takes on its sedimentary layers
deep in the wine-dark eyes of God
I settle to wander. All good drunks are liars.
Therefore, all lying drunks are good.

The bartender's not convinced. She frowns
and cuts me off. Outside, the orchestra rattles
the prelude to the morning, where I'll fawn
over pristine mysteries of sunlight and the riddles

of the hallway light: always illumined
even at my darkest. I will not find
a hanged man in the closet's vines.
Only hollow vessels and the sound of wind.

Streets are dark tonight without your love
to send me reeling anywhere but home
in this great hilled city I can't bring myself to leave.
I am never going to end this, April. Harm

will not fall. And through the buildings wind
sings songs of you. And at my window, leaves
wash up against the glass. No convenient end
is near. No April, as long as either of us lives

the end is far. It stretches out before me like the night.
The bars are all downhill from me. To stagger home
is ever a struggle for a man who wanders not.
Who staggers always home. What good is him?

XXIII.

Standing in the full glare of May Day splendour [Margaret] looked
thin, peaked. . .wide, staring, glassy like a crystal gazer's.
—HD

In Arkansas, the wind portends hard rain.
Never is the still heat of the summer broken
but for rain. So breeze came clipping and I ran
for shelter. But the rain came. I was stricken,

cold and soaked beneath the sky. A flash
flood, underneath God's sky, and I remember
that arch-poetic word: your *flesh,*
the weakness of the flesh. How frail. How slender

were your arms. How brown your eyes how thick
your smile was, trembling lips. I shiver.
Could it be the rain or you? On times I think
of you, I always wonder if it's possible to sever

a memory from whatever cause reminds.
How rain will always bring you back again,
or whatever omens that the Good Lord sends.
For instance, how the wind portends hard rain.

XXIV.

*I open this letter once more to affirm the belief and right in what I
am doing.*
— MC

Your last words were what caused us to continue
(*I was sick that day, sick in the head*)
avalanched in some broad sweep by you
(*A puddle of black milk to dip our bread*)

O girl of mine who won't exist.
(*I was sick that day, sick in the head*)
A tumor in the Lord's way bloomed (*to some extent
if the wound is closed, the blood has all been shed*)

like cold light racing through the peaks
(*I was sick that day, sick in the head*)
or a toppled wicker basket, as the dawn breaks:
eventually all light cannot be held.

I was sick that day, sick in the head
(*I was sick that day, sick in the head*)
policing myself at the foot of the hospital bed.
(*It wasn't anything at all you said*)

You were too beautiful ever to be killed
(*I was sick that day, sick in the head*)
A blurry vision through a pint of milk.
(*There is a sort of paint that must be spilled*)

The sun through small brown whiskey floods.
(*I was sick that day, sick in the head.*)
(*Asked only for some cleaner blood.*)
(*Was delivered whole to you instead.*)

XXV.

*I think I have answered your last letter several times, but it was a
very nice one so I'll do it over again.*
—EP

The shadow of the girl beyond the wall
where once her form had cast its silhouette
as if projected on a screen, or, well,
a figure in relief, and tiered like minarets.

The shadow, beyond the hallway, of the girl,
curling the champagne flute against her lips.
The shadow in a window where a gale
cascades the curtains. In the corner, wherein slips

the shadow of the girl. Half-dozen empty bottles
of champagne along the window mark her years
of weeks of nights. Her teeth were bitter
at her lips—which I have ceased to taste. Are yours

O Margaret, stained as hers, with wine?
The shadow of the shadow of the girl. Is lovely
now, as blank and shapeless as the shadows when
the walls were darkened still, the girl above me.

XXVI.

*Catullus rather haunts this small nib of earth, I wish I had more of
him, intact, haunting my ~~ear~~ head. . .So there's another ~~book to be
manufactured~~ book to be arranged.*
—EP

These are old songs that won't repeat.
The girl from Carthage climbs atop the pyre,
her woman weeping. How could Virgil put
in what dead tongue this loose and mournful choir?

But these lamentful songs resound, a tone
that must have haunted you that evening when
you sat and played that sad and dismal tune
and watched the late-day shadows wane.

What did your poet promise he would find
if only you would pay his room and board?
A symphony that only you could fund?
One shouldn't pay the rent to lease a bard.

These distinctions echo loudest sotto voce,
uncorrected whispers of old Greek.
But not the sea surge. Not the voices
of the muse. Merely the warbled streak

of print, correcting print, correcting print.
That older way of writing too unchaste.
You saw the words as sharpened to a point:
the gunshot in the middle of your chest.

XXVII.

*Margaret liked having you in Paris. I don't know that anything
would have kept her.*
—EP

Words worn and weary and I look out
over Arkansas from my seventh story office
and think of you. I neither sleep nor eat.
Only drink, and admire the calming effect

of the great hilled city that cascades below.
Through the mountains of the causeway,
Margaret, cold wind moans and bellows
songs of you. Leave me beverage to soothsay

times of you when I descended
into the hell we made for one another.
It's not excessive to say that you reminded
me of hell. Or heaven. Although neither

strike me as belonging to someone who could
strike against the cold space of her heart
and open that space to the equally cold
June evening in a gasp that anyone could hear

on the street below. From the seventh floor
I watch the students swarm like locusts,
swirling and joining with rhythmic flare
and a happiness that I no longer locate

as belonging to a man. Or girl. Unmaking
of a life is unfathomably thin, as cold as glass.
Against the window panel's edge, thin masking.
Far below, the rows of students pass.

XXVIII.

Walter's technique was "exquisite. . .his music flowing like water, a
technique that Debussy said he himself couldn't cope with."
—Hilda Doolittle

April woke and went about her day.
But over the years so much had changed.
At her desk, she wrote of different ways to die
instead of dreaming up new songs to sing.

In her neat one-bedroom she'd arrayed
the walls with clipped-out words—a phrase
or two of mine I wrote for her. She read
less now than ever. Ink became dim frieze,

a band of black around her walls. A band,
just like her world, grown tighter
by day as she retreated to an empty, bland
life unfulfilled. And every note I wrote her

to tell her of my love, each decorated verse
of inexorable, impenetrable lust
reminded her that she no longer wrote. And worse:
that I could send her in retreat. Wounded, she'd list

new ways to die. Of course she never meant
that any of these words be found.
But in each line, some truth. April, this climate
is as mine. So even if you think I don't, I understand.

XXIX.

All these accounts touched on the truth, though they discerned only
the brighter spots in the galaxy of Margaret's motivation.
—OP and RS

O quiet skies which drown in the dawn
and the certain silences of soft-red, violet,
gray. The gray belongs to me alone,
I think. But that is a stupid thought,

I think again, drowning among the smoke
of an infinitely dirty cigarette
I light to bring you off me, and I choke
whatever breath you smothered there on that

gray day you walked the water's edge.
Did you stare at your reflection, chopped among
the waves, where each reverberating ridge
brought each separate part of you along,

back to the breakers? So you broke.
And so you threw the whole of you away.
This is all I think of while I smoke
and flecks of light come breaking through the gray.

XXX.

Dorothy has a horrible cough which I don't in the least like, and for eight cents I'd bring her down into the sun.
—EP

A bird in the house is an omen of death
But death follows all things. All things in life
are omens of death. There is no dearth
of ill omen. The reappearance of a leaf

was omen to Eliot, who lamented and muttered
of rebirth and fertility. Even the spring
was an omen of death! Not that it matters
but Eliot died. All die. Some hang by a string.

Some are bent from being in one fell swoop.
Perhaps it's worse if there's time to prepare
April noticed firsthand as the illness swept
across her mother in that high-backed chair

where she watched her children on Christmas
opening gifts. And later in that hospice bed
where, one dark morning, she was christened
into the abyss. I mean, that is, the abyss of the dead.

April's father woke her early with the news.
They placed on the door a funereal wreath.
What departs from us will not again come near.
A bird in the house is an omen of death.

XXXI.

You will come over here, won't you, if Paris is out of tune. "Lon-
don" is about ready to begin.
—EP

Below the hemisphere that will divide
discord from sleep, the world is green
and innocent. This morning shocks of rain invade
your windows. Across the living room you grin

but April, hands will not unfold me. Water
gutters through the city, deep and wide, and snow
puddles under passing cars, and later
Chicago stretches high its roofs above. Below

a thick sky, I'm helpless as you wander
through the choices: anything that you could
promise. April. Silhouettes against your window
wait for wind, for me to say: *I wouldn't want the world*

you have to offer here, this cold Chicago street.
What can you give me? Is there anything
I love? The open form. The poems of the modernists.
The echoing of gunfire which portends to bring

a revolution. Remember the judgment of Paris: Peace
or Grace or Empires? Not even empires. Only beauty,
April, though yours fled at that rushed pace
you chose. But I chose nothing. Only you. My duty

was to you. A light shines in a window floors above
and somehow thunder echoes down below.
This still and simple vision's all I have.
A frozen wind blows frozen winter snow.

XXXII.

*Personally I'm keeping my head thru' the maelstrom because I must
make a perfect sapphic ode before I pass on. That sort of anchor
holds.*
— EP

Lost in England, lost among my words,
I turned to you, O old gray beard
to find a pen to fall, in lieu of sword.
I found, instead, another failing bard

paired with a girl — like April — whom you loved
not, or not enough as she'd have had
you love. In the 14-story building where I lived
I counted the seconds for a penny to hit *hard*

the pavement below my fourth floor flat.
Or from the empty flat 10 floors above
I'd watch the rain unfold and splatter
on the ground. I thought of love

as you spoke of love in my favorite of your poems:
I will not spoil my sheath with lesser light.
Old light. Less light. A frost among the spume,
as if there could be frost there, and, as if, of late

it being frost could make less severe my doubt.
I know then how you felt, wringing your hands
among the Sirmione sun, to bring a drought
of darkness over all your years. O there she stands

as if alive, in portrait on my book
as I lie sleepless three nights four nights five.
There on my bookshelf, tell me Ezra, look:
is that your Margaret, Margaret still alive?

XXXIII.

I feel bold as a lion when I issue forth upon the cliffs and swear gently at the snow on the distant hills.
—EP

Will they lock me someday in a cage?
Not for the crimes, the crimes for which I alone
can atone. Like Achilles, he began to us with rage.
He ends: *Let the Gods forgive what I have done.*

I knew a British man who said to me:
I find him impossibly, interminably dense.
It's hard to say I disagree
but Ezra, what does that say about me? O, cleanse

me in the filth that was your soul. And O,
my soul's as stained by her as yours.
Tell me what there's left for me to do
except continue with the poem, of course.

XXXIV.

I feel like a swine eating its aesthetic head off.
—EP

It is not about the man himself.
His words like the blade of a scythe
can no longer haunt us. We are safe
from harm. He has been made scarce.

So where does that leave us, you and I,
as the evening stretches out, a broad
moon, flat and dumb against the sky,
a puddle of black milk to dip our bread?

There is a creature of our own creation,
then, behind whom we can no longer hide.
My Irish friend tells me I'm a fascist, a notion
I wish could be easily, swiftly decried

with a wave of a politick hand. Instead
I stood side by side with Pound in London
waiting and weeping where sleepless I stood
wrapped in a clean, white, dreamless linen

wishing for God to come and calmly press
me into your pages, neatly, Margaret Cravens
(who is no longer dead). My clasped hand prays
weeping sleepless five nights six nights seven

for any god to come with a mighty palm
and crush the unrighteous me for to feed
the soul. I would be burnt offering. Would be alm.
This, my bloodless, sleepless need.

I forgot there *was* a Pound. Forgot the girl
shot through her chest that summer afternoon.
But I remembered you by your toes, the way they'd curl.
I measured the days by if I would see you soon.

XXXV.

I am returned to the momentous problem of saying poetically that
the sky is composed of sheet sapphire and cotton wool.
—EP

I have seen a beautiful sky. Not yours.
The swollen, wriggled morning bleak.
I have seen nights in your arms. Not years.
Where in the windowpane, the black

of a moonless sky brightens its hourly pace
and weakens, I can't help but wonder
if the south you made for him stank piss
and did you sleep beside where he would wander,

tuning that unheard dirge you played
at that last toast and tea you took, for
all this, our western thought? O plaid
and latticed shadows of the moon! So far

I know only of the wind that passed
through parts of you the heart mistook
for lung. In brief and early night, you paused:
Down came the lights. Down, down you shook.

XXXVI.

I'm sorry you [have] been disappointed in matters of estate, but the grief is "purely platonic," at least I hope it is.
—EP

Even with all her arms to weave,
April's stories still upset the gods.
Broken fragments. Legs she waved.
An arm. A whim. Her shattered goods

where in a corner shadows sway.
The doorway couldn't hold
and so she fell. I found her that way,
supine. Beautiful. All legs. I held

each bright and easy ankle, more
to beautify in inches each red joint.
Everything was particles. Her
various unravelings, spun to this point

where belly up and in the corner
they laid her flat against the ground.
I hid her in my arms: this girl I carried
off to where she couldn't be unwound.

XXXVII.

We need conspirators, if the country is to be Guy Fawked into an artistic paradise.
—EP

Explosions shook the walls of Edgeware Road
the summer just after I'd returned
to Indiana. On the internet I read
of unzipped shells of buses, tunnels turned

to rubble. But O the world began to bomb
itself to pieces long before I was born.
Achilles rests in a deep and fitful tomb,
the tendons at his ankles torn.

I'm twenty-six this year. My hair's begun
to gray, though mine is not a difficult life.
Before a mirror, I run my hand again
and count each white strand: leaf by leaf by leaf.

April, did you lose someone you loved when cars
were blown to bits in the shadows of late June?
I had no one there I really loved because
I couldn't afford to travel zone to zone

except to see you. So when I finally heard
about these bombs so close to our former home,
I imagined at every jolt it was *your* blood.
Recalled your death. It felt about the same.

XXXVIII.

If you are coming back, come to me.
—WR

4th of July. Serene and patterned sky.
Falling tears of flame. Against you, flush,
a door wedged shut, I turn and say
You are the widened night. The rockets flash

and rend the sky in simple verticals,
planned and elegant in gold, green, bronze
to break apart the miserable, vestigial
sounds of summer. Across the breeze

we too begin to trickle where we'll fall
from all our catapulting skyward, to dissipate
the wattles of these flashes, which, however full,
will culminate. And then recede. And then depart.

XXXIX.

*The spring of 1912 must have seemed like a nightmare of desertion
to Margaret.*
—OP and RS

Ariadne, spin me in the pageant
of what-can-be-lost. Whatever turns I make
are plaid with layers of decisions. Pregnant
with indecisions. Each wall I pass, I leave a mark

to trace me back by: trails of bread
which lead me wrong. Within this nightmare, all
are *blameless*, lost though we be. Yet broad
as it seems: all are *responsible*.

These imagined tragedies are all we know of how
to separate what consequences *mean*.
I wake up, gasping, nonetheless. I know
I can never follow you to sleep. A man

who traces someone's thread will undermine
whatever *cause* unfurled her spool,
and further, how that cause might be *determined*.
In any case, you watched me set my whitened sail

against the sky. I set it broad and high against the wind.
White, which meant victorious. I left the way I came.
You were waiting for my ship to come to land.
It never did. I was departing home.

XL.

Come over here to London & put yourself under my protection if
you can't manage it any other way.
—EP

When we're removed from this foul congress
of icicles, the wires sheathed in ice will fall.
Trees fall. Sky won't hold. Apartheid congress
of the trees and sky. So light bulbs wisp and fail,

all flickering. Candles languish in the limits
of the limitlessness of fire. In an ice storm
falling limbs can cause such passive damage
I didn't even notice you were dying, strewn

some seven hundred miles removed
from all this ice. The tile floor quickens
all around you. Flecks of orange walls remind
that you are still alive, as you allow to darken

all these walls, return to sleep. Your family waits
in stiff blue chairs to find out what it was you saw.
A shroud of lake to wrap you quiet?
Knives to dissipate the clouds? Did you

not realize what smothered you was busy
weighing everything around me? Soaped
the sky is low. The moon fulfills its duty
in the sidewalk's wraith. The world is sapped

of all its sun. A veil of ghosts surrounds.
The sun is dying. Pay attention: the sky
is burning. All around me, sounds
of branches, but far north there's no reply.

No words arrive: recovery or funeral?
Your world could never end in ice. The wet
and slow release is far too heavy to be final.

To have any kind of weight.

XLI.

*She should have married. Then it would have been all right. Then
she wouldn't have been a virgin, gone mad, simply, like Cassandra.*
—HD

These swines, a drunkard they yclep'd me.
Or so the words from Hamlet echo now.
The dinge of sadness has not yet eclipsed me,
Margaret, I think you'd be indifferent to know,

since this is what you grappled with disinterestedly
in the cradle of a poet's thoughts for you
which, in your book, dissociated, lie
unspoken in — it seems to me — plain view.

April can stand for you, and I for your man
renowned in letters. So it strikes me, when
cradled in my arms, she let that moan
escape her teeth, unclothed and wan

and sick to death of her own doubts and said:
*You write enough for both of us, but that
is one of us too many.* And in that hostel, sad
while I wandered, who presumes to know her thoughts

but me? What meaning can I claim from her death
or what she sought in me? Or what gives voice
to a panicked woman, struggling against a dearth
of what she counted as acclaim? There is no vice

in ambition, Margaret. Only in despair, that worst
of sins, which means surrender at the hands
of god. Who sees all. Who saw all at the first.
Who all things living and unliving comprehends.

It's only in despair that I guess at — and guess wrongly —
what lies between the words your letters show.
All I can do is guess, and will guess wrongly

44

as the quote from Shakespeare will attest to now.

XLII.

So I can't see that I'm in any way subjected to the slings & arrows
of outrageous fortune.
—EP

My first thought was, she loved me once.
My second was, the mystery of why—
that pressing question, terrifying since
she left at last in such a patronizing way.

Her letter on the nightstand. . .or the letters
mouthed against my shoulder on the train,
spelling out the London evening. Later
we climbed my narrow bed to strain

our bodies against the limits of that space.
She worried, as if there were a question whether
I could let that brilliant and lovely creature face
even a week without me, let her softness wither.

Except, I did. If I'm honest—and what danger
is there now in being honest (except for what
admitting that would mean, no longer
able to beg off those devotions I would write

to appease her in her shell of self-defeat)
she is the only girl I loved—or else, she *was*.
I'm glad I can't—if I wanted—tell her how I felt,
that she can't insist that I enumerate the ways.

Understand: she was beautiful, as all girls are,
but *beautiful*, thick eyes, the color of dark smoke,
quick patterns that defined her tangled hair,
and a throat that swelled with every word she spoke.

Because I am without her, now I long
for her. Because I am without. My first
thought was, she loved me once. Could I be wrong?

Could I be wrong? As if that would be worse.

XLIII.

Yes, O fountain of my salvation.
—EP

What terrible beasts our bodies are. And once
O April, in agony in bed my body buckt.
Love's slow turn in my stomach, and I winced
and all the words I had for you fell black.

There is a hell and heaven, us between,
a circle on the outmost ring of hell.
And O the days grow long and sharp and mean
in this dim and shadowed circle where we dwell.

Your body was my temple, feet my altar.
I should have brought my body to your pyre.
There was nowhere for my offering, much later
when I'd married my petitions to your fire.

XLIV.

She saw that she would be left behind, the sole bohemian in an
altered Paris.
—OP and RS

I never learned the names of ferns or birds
or the gradations or the scalloping of shells
along the seashore—This is what I told my third
girl: all I know is blood collects within my soul.

come winter, which means, for her
no other blood will flow. Not for me,
not her, regardless whether I'd prefer
it to. The simple fact: death comes in three.

I count them for her: April, Margaret, me
at last, as days ooze past and nights grow thin
and in the dark and flashing neon, we
lean close to one another. Even then

I am uncreated by this rule of thirds.
Each death creates another third. Each death
collapses with an overwhelming thud,
resounds and echoes and I am quite loath

to continue with such trivial things as love.
Margaret was the second when I found
her book, when April took her leave
from me. I need you, Margaret, as my friend,

my second. How else could I reason through
what seems even now so hard to see—
how she could do what came so easily to you
and—to myself? Of course. Death comes in three.

XLV.

The tables sort of emerge from the wreckage.
—EP

The pulse of the world is in my footsteps
as I pace the sidewalk, gaze over the ledge
at the railroad track below. I let my feet stop
where the railing rises and defines the edge.

So far below to my inevitable end, April, you
are not the reason I am here. No, not
to try to understand or glean some clue
how disappointment could have brought

you to such an edge. I know how in a mind
one word repeats and echoes. A revision:
one word struck against the page. One act to mend
a life which awakens in you now revulsion.

How liberating to gaze down very far
and see only vast and empty space can keep
you from erasure. Empty space, and fear,
a fear which creeps along my spine. Which creeps

even as I start to climb the rail and feel
the freeness of that space—not the ethereal
emptiness you left me. No. A void that's *real*
and no less empty. The sublime. The immaterial.

The tall weeds look like grass below. A whistle
sounds, a passenger train which brings it guests
along to someplace I will never go. A vessel
far below which brings to me its ghosts.

I stand and wait for some decision. None
arrives. Just so I'm clear, I didn't come to grieve.
I came so far above the tracks to be alone.
When the train comes into sight, I leave.

XLVI.

I can only make out enough of the enclosed to see that your friend
[Mrs. Lowes] is charming. BUT her handwriting is worse than
yours.
—EP

We are coming so close to the end.
These words — these shambolic words —
will crumble us as we drift from land
to whatever Avalon we've made. As hard

as it is to put you away, my Margaret,
lie quiet beside your Ezra on my shelf.
These notes I've spilled along your margins
are the ribbonings you made yourself.

Or of yourself, spread on your wall,
red patternings of you, unraveled.
A sort of triumph of a woman's will.
Preludes to the trumpets he would revel

of you upon a lotus, dead and laughing.
This was the agony you made for us:
years of drought and weeks of fasting
until our pace of grief had been misused.

When in a pond or glass, I see your ghost
behind me, and I turn to speak
you always disappear, deep in a gust
of wind. Or were you always just a speck

to be removed from mine eye before
I could proceed? Should I have viewed
you darkly through a lens, afar
astray the path that you and April veered

from all of us who loved you, Margaret? No.
Here begin my dreams of you to end. Unless

I could reimagine you just *so*.
Leave you for the reader to undress.

XLVII.

I am trying to do a long poem, much more important than anything
I've yet attempted, but that's as far as it goes
—EP

My girl appears to me with eyes of smoke,
speaks softly through a dream. Her hair
curls down her cheek. It trembles as she speaks.
Throat soft, she murmurs. Murmurs here

and there of time lost spent. I wander lonely
echoes of her back. Trace down her spine
to find her waist. I kiss her, leaning
slight against her hips. We spin, I spin

my girl and dance her to the bed.
She settles, and her breasts relax
to settle where she settles. Oh, it's not so bad
to hold her. Even, touch her where she likes.

She is not dead. She has not died,
though we both will someday soon.
As for now, we'll find our peace inside
the quiet torment of the arms of sin.

XLVIII.

I feel (10th time I've used that word in this epistle) a bit too light for
a weather-vane.
—EP

What has he ever done, I can hear you ask.
Margaret, the answer impossible, even
to begin to devise. In beginning, risk
itself is too severe—to venture even

and fail blandly, generally—even then
the room will gape, stripped of all cover.
Oh and the days grow long and pale and thin,
the words in every sense impossible to recover.

I would answer, I suppose: I spend my days
pushing words around until they fit,
hoping to awaken their invisible arrays.
No luck. The page stays blank, and gray, and flat.

What has he ever done? There's still that matter.
I suppose my best response would be this poem.
It's *you* I've made. And Margaret, in this meter,
I wish that you could see what you've become.

XLIX.

*My Dear Child: Pardon the paternal tone of the greeting but I shall
use it just as long as you find it necessary to allude to me as "the au-
thor". . .I happen to have written a prose book, but I also have cooked
food & made salads.*
—EP

I always wrote with my bedroom door
open to her voice, so she could call
for me to serenade her. April, my dear,
it kept me from that lonely cell

of writing, three floors up, removed
from the ear, the critical ear of time.
I sent you letters. Words. I waved
the palms of poesy at your passing team

of mules (ahem). Now I write only to the blank
and silent rooms which wall me. Which
won't offer any hint to where these words will rank
among my history of words. They will not. Watch.

L.

Write to me, dear, and I will answer as best I can. I won't say,
"don't write me trivial things," but write to [me] gravely for a little.
—EP

Her birthday passes. I remember only slightly
the way we were before the fall.
There is a song called Sluttering
I never played for her, but I recall

the verse before it's sung: *This is the story*
you won't tell the kids we'll never have.
Tonight, March 23rd is starry,
and, though March 23rd, too cold by half.

And I'm not exactly glad that April's gone
but if she had to leave then it was probably best.
But on these days I'm left to understand alone
what is unanswerable, I miss her most.

I was a desert once. She left me desert.
Nothing hardly ever grows.
But any time a blade appears, I'll bear it.
Nothing hardly ever grows.

LI.

You who know how to express things in words, I should be glad if
you would write a letter to my aunt. . .just from one who has seen
me lately and knew that all was well with me at the last.
— MC

My heart is a grain of salt, she said, *and these*
*are all the things dead drunk. . .*And so I vanished.
April was light with half-air. Collecting in her eyes:
a simple puddle of transmission fluid. Famished

I hungered, pawing at her gutters. *Justice,*
she said, inexorable. *Hunger,* she said, unwavering.
And so I slept three days away, an autumn Jesus.
Hugely arrayed with leaves in need of watering —

which click like straw — along this road I cross
to find her apartment, my feet are hands
on dry, white paper, fishing through the loose
and windy covering of words. Rather than

potential, what remains of us is *possibility.*
I go downhill to find her when I walk,
meaning I lived above her always. Unstably
balanced, footsteps hush across the wake

of dead leaves strewn along her road. She waited
for me, curled in sofa, pencil in her ear, reporting
on the sighs of water through the rocks of wilted
artificial fountains. *Sirens in the trees, repeating,*

she said. Meaning: *Wreck me on the rocks.*
Meaning: officers are on their way to find me guilty
for all the crimes I owe, those nights spent wrecked
upon her rocks. The rain streams through that gully

where I dried up long ago. The clean and August rain
which softens leaves has long been vanquished

by that drought, too dry, too loose itself. Again
to loose itself again. And so I vanished.

LII.

*One feels good and relieved to be human once in awhile. I have felt
the necessity of it these days.*
—WR

Here the road to Damascus comes
like cold. Like winter from autumn,
red and ember at its very core.
Of lust. Polices lust with solemn,

justifying words: *Had we intermediates
and time.* Our poetry is politics. The mind
in the act of governing what it premeditates.
What the act of revision never mends:

the overwhelming need to be tucked in
each night, and led where anyone can bleed
(and *anyone* can bleed). But fiction
is something *anyone* can write, its bald-

faced lies, and Einstein greater than the Greeks.
Wide-eyed, I neared Damascus, whence we came.
Did you think—and April, think before you speak—
the first thing that we saw would be the same?

We rest of us who are not yet ready for such damp white-petaled beatitude may as well continue with our **paradis** terrestre.
—EP

The whole midwest is wooden crosses
stapled to the median. Chalk-monuments
to gradients of our various losses
however bleak. However minimal.

You were from Indiana where I spent
the better part of four years learning
how to disappear from myself. How to respond
calmly to a sea of human yearning —

though the sea is far from Indiana. Pain
is existence, goes the Buddha. Goes
down the litany of sacred texts again,
my finger, tracing, but the list just grows

of words which can not save me from —
from what? The only one I'd ask is you
who can not give me words. But perhaps, a frame?
Geoff Brock taught me "The Moon and the Yew

Tree" — *the O-gape of despair.* The shape,
the roundness of that letter's whole. The hole
into which the constant danger of *to slip*
is overwhelming. Teeth of Melville's whale,

jungle of Conrad's darkness, water
on a red, dry rock. But I am from Wisconsin.
My father's father was a Chinese waiter.
My mother's was a Belgian mutt. A cancer

waits on either side. O Margaret Cravens,
you aren't the only one who died that night —
the people around you too, that coven
of spirits running from their past. The light

of western Europe was merely marsh gas,
a will o' the wisp of your own design
you chased for the chance at one last gasp
of anything but this past where I descend,

banal and flat. American as America can be —
a stable of ghosts of little importance
except to those who came to know them, by and by.
Margaret, I can see now your impertinence

toward that mortal coil you shuffled off,
joining yourself, calm, to the calm June sky —
better to die by gunshot than by ragged cough.
But Margaret — Margaret, I am not ready to die.

A NOTE ABOUT THE AUTHOR

Chris Wong's work has appeared in a number of journals, including *Art Amiss, Caffeine Destiny* and the *Shadyside Review*. He currently lives in Fayetteville, AR where he teaches English at the University of Arkansas.

www.ingramcontent.com/pod-product-compliance
Lightning Source LLC
Chambersburg PA
CBHW072049040426
42447CB00012BB/3074